P9-DBO-921

THE BIBLE CURE® FOR

DEPRESSION AND ANXIETY

DON COLBERT, M.D.

Living in Health–-Body, Mind and Spirit

THE BIBLE CURE FOR DEPRESSION AND ANXIETY
by Don Colbert, M.D.
Published by Siloam Press
A part of Strang Communications Company
600 Rinehart Road
Lake Mary, Florida 32746
www.siloampress.com

Library of Congress Catalog Card Number:
99-74596

International Standard Book Number:
0-88419-650-X

01 02 03 04   10 9 8 7 6
Printed in the United States of America

Joy Instead of Sadness

The secret is out—*even Christians get depressed.* Unfortunately, Christian people often feel that they must hide their pain and pretend that nothing is wrong. This act in itself can make their condition much worse and more difficult to overcome. If you are battling with depression, or if someone in your physical or spiritual family is suffering from depression, I can confidently tell you that there is hope for you.

You or a loved one may feel depressed or anxious at the moment, but you took an important first step toward complete healing, health and joy when you picked up this booklet. As a caring Christian and as a medical doctor, I wrote this book specifically to help you and those you love take hold of what Jesus called "inexpressible joy" (this must surely be the opposite of depression, an "inexpressible sadness").

The apostle Peter said that this kind of joy stems from our love for Jesus Christ: "You love him even though you have never seen him. Though you do not see him, you trust him; and even now you are happy with a glorious, inexpressible joy" (1 Pet. 1:8).

This Bible Cure booklet will help you move from depression to happiness and from worry to peace of mind. Welcome to yet another hope-filled booklet in the Bible Cure series developed by Siloam Press to help you know how to keep the temple of your body fit and healthy. In this series of booklets, you will

uncover God's divine plan of health
for body, soul and spirit
through modern medicine, good nutrition
and the medicinal power
of Scripture and prayer.

This booklet is filled with powerful promises of God from the Bible that will help you focus on the healing power of God. The proven principles, truths and guidelines in these passages anchor the practical and medical insights also contained in this booklet. They will effectively focus your prayers, thoughts and actions so you can step into God's plan of divine health for you—a plan that includes victory over depression and anxiety.

In this Bible Cure booklet you will discover chapters on:

I pray that these spiritual and practical suggestions for health, nutrition and fitness will bring wholeness to your life, increase your spiritual understanding and strengthen your ability to worship and serve God.

—DON COLBERT, M.D.

A BIBLE CURE PRAYER
FOR YOU

Heavenly Father, I ask in the name of Jesus that You would open my heart and mind to the truth and absolute power of Your Word, the Bible. Give me supernatural hope and total assurance that if I come to You with my burdens, then You can and will help me totally overcome depression or prevent it altogether. Give me the courage and the ability to apply everything I learn to my own life so I can live in complete victory over fear, anxiety and worry. Thank You, Father. I give You all of the glory and praise for my healing and victory, in the name of my Healer, Jesus Christ. Amen.

Chapter 1

Joy Instead of Sadness

L et me get right to the point: If you feel depressed at this very moment, *you don't have to stay depressed.* Take courage because *The Bible Cure for Depression and Anxiety* will give you positive natural and spiritual steps to help you overcome depression, sadness, anxiety and worry. You can start this very minute to move from the "pit of pain" to the plain of stability, wholeness and peace of mind.

It is normal for people to feel "down" or to have the "blues" when they experience a sad circumstance such as the death of a loved one or friend, the loss of a job, a divorce, separation or some other significant loss. However, anyone who experiences continued depression without any

1

recognizable cause should know that this may be a warning sign of major depression an affliction that affects millions of people around the world. This Bible Cure booklet will help you replace depression—and even sadness with God's joy.

The good news is that you can overcome depression. God has provided you with resources in both the natural and spiritual realms to defeat depression and anxiety. As you take the positive steps outlined in this booklet, hope should begin to replace depression and inner peace will overcome anxiety. (Note: If your depression persists or deepens, consult a physician, pastor or Christian counselor before you take any steps. At times even the strongest ones among us need a helping hand to climb over an obstacle.)

> *Don't worry about anything; insead, pray about everything. Tell God what you need, and thank him for all he has done. If you do this, you will experience God's peace, which is far more wonderful than the human mind can understand. His peace will guard your hearts and minds as you live in Christ Jesus.*
> —PHILIPPIANS 4:6–7

Depression is a global problem. One in six people around the world will suffer from major depression at some point during their lives. It has been estimated that by the year 2020 depression will be the greatest disability worldwide.[1]

Are You Depressed?

A self-test

If you check "yes" to more than two of the following questions, you may well be depressed. Consult your physician, pastoral counselor or a mental health professional and take the positive steps they recommend along with the helping resources you choose in this book.

1. Much of the time, do you feel . . .

Sad?	❑ Yes	❑ No
Lethargic?	❑ Yes	❑ No
Pessimistic?	❑ Yes	❑ No
Hopeless?	❑ Yes	❑ No
Worthless?	❑ Yes	❑ No
Helpless?	❑ Yes	❑ No

2. Do you often . . .

❑ Have difficulty making decisions?

❑ Have trouble concentrating?
❑ Have memory problems?

3. Lately, have you . . .

❑ Lost interest in things that used to give you pleasure?
❑ Had problems at work or in school?
❑ Had problems with your family or friends?
❑ Isolated yourself from others? Or wanted to?
❑ Felt that you have no energy?
❑ Felt restless and irritable?
❑ Had trouble falling asleep, staying asleep or getting up in the morning?
❑ Lost your appetite or gained weight?
❑ Experienced persistent headaches, stomachaches, backaches and muscle or joint pains?
❑ Been drinking more alcohol than normal?
❑ Been taking more mood-altering drugs than you used to?
❑ Engaged in risky behavior such as not wearing a seat belt or crossing streets without looking?
❑ Been thinking about death or your funeral?
❑ Been hurting yourself?[2]

Today in the U.S. and in many other parts of the world we are experiencing an epidemic of stress.

Too much stress leads to distress, which eventually leads to depression. Excessive stress decreases the adrenal hormone DHEA, a hormone that actually protects us from the effects of stress.

Are You Stressed Out?

Your stress scale

Look up stress-producing changes in your life in the following table and see how stressed out you really are. Add up your score from the stressful events you have experienced over the past twelve months.

Stress Event Values

1.	Death of Spouse	100
2.	Divorce	60
3.	Menopause	60
4.	Separation from a partner	60
5.	Jail term or probation	60
6.	Death of a close family member other than spouse	60
7.	Serious personal injury or illness	45
8.	Marriage or establishing life partnership	45
9.	Fired at work	45
10.	Marital or relationship reconciliation	40

11.	Retirement	40
12.	Change in health of an immediate family member	40
13.	Work more than forty hours a week	35
14.	Pregnancy or causing pregnancy	35
15.	Sex difficulties	35
16.	Gain of new family member	35
17.	Change in business or work role	35
18.	Change in financial state	35
19.	Death of close friend (not a family member)	30
20.	Change in number of arguments with spouse	30
21.	Mortgage or loan for financial purposes	25
22.	Foreclosure of mortgage or loan	25
23.	Sleep less than eight hours per night	25
24.	Change in responsibilities at work	25
25.	Trouble with in-laws or children	25
26.	Outstanding personal achievement	25
27.	Spouse begins or stops work	20
28.	Begin or end school	20
29.	Change in living conditions (visitors in the home, change in roommates, remodeling house)	20
30.	Change in personal habits (diet, exercise, smoking)	20

31.	Chronic allergies	20
32.	Trouble with boss	20
33.	Change in work hours or conditions	15
34.	Moving to new residence	15
35.	Presently in premenstrual period	15
36.	Change in schools	15
37.	Change in religious activities	15
38.	Change in social activities (more or less than before)	15
39.	Minor financial loan	10
40.	Change in frequency of family get-togethers	10
41.	Vacation	10
42.	Presently in winter holiday season	10
43.	Minor violation of the law	5

TOTAL SCORE:_____

Looking at the last twelve months of changes in your life may surprise you. Major changes in your life have effects that last for long periods of time. A life crisis is like dropping a rock into a pond. After the initial splash, you will experience additional ripples of stress—and these ripples may last for at least a year.

If your total stress score over the last twelve

months is 250 or greater, you may be feeling over-stressed, even if you are normally stress tolerant. Persons with a low tolerance for stress may be overstressed at levels beginning at 150.

Overstress can make you sick. Carrying too heavy a load of stress is like running your car engine full throttle without letting up, or like leaving your toaster stuck in the on position. Sooner or later, something will break, burn up or melt down—and that something might be you! What breaks depends on where the weak links, or the weaknesses, are in your physical body. This will be largely due to inherited characteristics.[3]

Stress causes an increase in *cortisol levels*. Too much cortisol can lead to depression, insomnia and anxiety. One of the main reasons we see such an epidemic of depression in the U.S.

> *I am leaving you with a gift peace of mind and heart. And the peace I give isn't like the peace the world gives. So don't be troubled or afraid.*
> —JOHN 14:27

is that so many Americans are stressed out. This leads to increased levels of cortisol and decreased levels of the protective hormone DHEA, a state that eventually can cause major depression.

Reducing Stress

You can take the following steps immediately to reduce your stress:

Fix your attention on Jesus and not your problems.

Dwelling on your problems produces inner turmoil and blocks the power of Christ, the Prince of Peace, from comforting and calming you. Follow this Bible cure prescription:

> Therefore, since we are surrounded by such a huge crowd of witnesses to the life of faith, let us strip off every weight that slows us down, especially the sin that so easily hinders our progress. And let us run with endurance the race that God has set before us. We do this by keeping our eyes on Jesus, on whom our faith depends from start to finish. He was willing to die a shameful death on the cross because of the joy he knew would be his afterward. Now he is seated in the place of highest honor beside God's throne in heaven.
>
> —HEBREWS 12:1–2

Pray and thank God for all His blessings.

When stressed, you may tend to forget all that God has done and is doing in your life. Your blessings far outweigh any temporary crisis. As you pray for your needs, also thank God for His providential care: "So I tell you, don't worry about everyday life—whether you have enough food, drink, and clothes. Doesn't life consist of more than food and clothing? Look at the birds. They don't need to plant or harvest or put food in barns because your heavenly Father feeds them. And you are far more valuable to him than they are" (Matt. 6:25–26).

Eliminate negative thoughts by meditating on uplifting thoughts.

Scripture reveals that you become what you think. (See Proverbs 23:7, KJV.) Instead of dwelling on what stresses you, clean out negative thoughts with the eraser of joy-filled things as described in the Bible: "Always be full of joy in the Lord. I say it again—rejoice! . . . Don't worry about anything; instead, pray about everything. Tell God what you need, and thank him for all he has done. If you do this, you will experience God's peace, which is far more wonderful than the human mind can understand. His peace will guard your hearts and minds as you live in Christ Jesus. And now, dear brothers and sisters, let me say one more thing as I close this letter. Fix your thoughts on what is true and honorable and right. Think about things that are pure and lovely and admirable. Think about things that are excellent and worthy of praise" (Phil. 4:4, 6–8).

Three Types of Depression

Depression is very misunderstood, perhaps because it can affect all three parts of our being—spirit, soul and body. Any truly effective treatment for depression must address all three areas. Most of

> *And this same God who takes care of me will supply all your needs from his glorious riches, which have been given to us in Christ Jesus.*
> —PHILIPPIANS 4:19

the time depression begins in our emotional and mental realm. Then it begins to affect our physical bodies, and finally it begins to affect our spiritual man. At times, the problem actually begins in the body because of a chemical imbalance or some other natural cause, which we will discuss later on. In any case, God has very real answers for the problem.

11

There are three different forms of depression:

Depressive reaction—This usually occurs as a result of a traumatic event or situation in life. In this case, individuals experience normal feelings of depression. These people usually do not need medical treatment and may feel sad for about two weeks to six months. However, they would still feel better physically and emotionally by taking the vitamins and supplements mentioned later in this book. Although every person's sadness is very important, this kind of depression is usually very temporary.

Dysthymia—This is characterized by a prevailing feeling of sadness. This disorder has symptoms similar to depression, but the symptoms are less intense and last at least two years. With this form of depression, a person is depressed most of the day and has two or more of the following symptoms:

> *Those who live in the shelter of the Most High will find rest in the shadow of the Almighty. This I declare of the LORD: He alone is my refuge, my place of safety; he is my God, and I am trusting him.*
> —PSALM 91:1–2

- Poor appetite or overeating

- Insomnia or hypersomnia

- Low energy or fatigue

- Low self-esteem

- Poor concentration or difficulty making decisions

- Feelings of hopelessness

Major depressive illness—Major depression is an illness that can lead to an inability to function normally in society, and it can eventually lead to suicide. Major depression includes at least four of the following symptoms:

> *And now, dear brothers and sisters . . . fix your thoughts on what is true and honorable and right. Think about things that are pure and lovely and admirable. Think about things that are excellent and worthy of praise.*
> —PHILIPPIANS 4:8

The Symptoms of Major Depression

- Feelings of guilt, helplessness, hopelessness or worthlessness
- Persistent sadness and a pessimistic attitude
- Difficulty concentrating
- Loss of interest or pleasure in normal activities that would bring pleasure, including sex
- Insomnia, early morning awakenings or oversleeping
- Fatigue and lack of energy
- Weight loss or weight gain
- Slow movements and slow speech
- Suicidal thoughts
- Agitation and irritability

HEALTHFACT HEALTHFACT HEALTHFACT HEALTHFACT HEALTHFACT HEALTHFACT HEALTHFACT

Depression often begins in the early middle-age years; it is fairly common among the elderly. Almost half of the cases of depression among the elderly are misdiagnosed by the patient's primary care doctor.

Depression among children and adolescents has also increased dramatically in the last fifty years. Children are becoming depressed at an earlier age. During adolescence, almost twice as many boys as girls are diagnosed. And over half of youth diagnosed with depression have a recurrence within seven years.[4]

Depression also can occur because of physical rather than psychological factors. Anyone experiencing

> *Those who love your law have great peace and do not stumble.*
> —PSALM 119:165

depression should be tested to have organic factors ruled out. These include:

- Drug reactions
- Anemia
- Alcohol
- Diabetes
- Cancer
- Rheumatoid arthritis
- Low adrenal function
- Low thyroid function
- Nutritional deficiencies
- Illegal drug use
- Chronic pain
- Heart disease
- Sleep disturbances

Elderly patients are very often overlooked as being depressed. Often they are told that their loss of memory or sadness is a normal part of growing old, that it is simply early senile dementia, which may develop into Alzheimer's disease. Alzheimer's disease is characterized by loss of brain function, including impairment of memory, judgment, reasoning, speech and socialization. Rarely striking before the age of fifty, the progression of this disease may take from a few months to as many as five years before complete loss of cognitive function.

Depression in the elderly is reversible. However, senile dementia is not. It is vitally important to make the correct diagnosis in order to give such individuals the appropriate care.

> *You will keep in perfect peace all who trust in you, whose thoughts are fixed on you!*
> —Isaiah 26:3

Theories About Depression

Why do people become depressed? Many theories about depression exist, such as the following:

- Depression is anger turned inward.
- Depression is caused by loss, such as the loss of a loved one or the loss of a job.
- *The Learned Helplessness Theory* states that depression is caused by feelings of hopelessness and pessimism.[5]
- The *Monoamine Hypothesis* states that chemical imbalances cause depression,

such as imbalances of monoamine chemicals, which include serotonin, epinephrine and norepinephrine. These chemicals help the neurons in the nervous system transmit their electrical impulses properly. When an imbalance in these chemicals occur, mental health is affected adversely.[6]

I believe that there is some truth in all of the different theories on depression. However, I also believe that we need a solution that combines these theories in order to identify and eliminate the psychological factors as well as to correct imbalances in neurotransmitters in the brain. (A neurotransmitter is a substance that transmits nerve impulses across a synapse—the space between the junction of two nerve cells—much like a telephone wire transmits signals between two telephones. Neurotransmitters include serotonin, dopamine, GABA (gamma-aminobutyric acid), norepinephrine and epinephrine.

Antidepressants

Antidepressants such as Prozac, Zoloft, Paxil and other synthetic antidepressants are called selective serotonin reuptake inhibitors (SSRIs). These drugs allow the level of serotonin in the brain to remain high. Serotonin is very helpful in overcoming depression, as we will see later.

All types of depression have a common spiritual thread—the lack of God's joy in our lives. God promises to make our joy full. "I

> *Don't be troubled. You trust God, now trust in me.*
> —JOHN 14:1

have told you this so that you will be filled with my joy. Yes, your joy will overflow!" (John 15:11) One certain antidepressant in your life is God's Word. Trust His promise and seek His overflowing joy through:

- Reading the Bible cure scriptures throughout this book
- Asking to be filled with God's joy
- Telling others about the promise of His joy

Do not be discouraged. You are already making giant strides in being filled with His joy and freed from the spirit of depression and sadness.

Reducing Your Stress

List the top three stressors from your stress test.

   1. _____

   2. _____

   3. _____

List any factors of which you are aware that may contribute to depression.

   1. _____

   2. _____

   3. _____

List three ways you can reduce stress in these areas of your life.

   1. _____

   2. _____

   3. _____

Chapter 2

Peace Instead
of Anxiety

D epression and anxiety are often companions. Any person who is depressed may also experience symptoms associated with anxiety.

- About 80 percent of depressed individuals suffer psychological anxiety symptoms: unrealistic apprehension, fears, worry, agitation, irritability or panic attacks.
- Some 60 percent of people with depression experience anxiety-related physical symptoms: headaches, irritable bowel syndrome, chronic fatigue and chronic pain.
- Approximately 65 percent of depression sufferers experience sleep disturbances.

About 20 percent feel agitated.
- Some 25 percent experience phobia.
- Approximately 17 percent report general-ized anxiety symptoms.
- About 10 percent suffer panic attacks.[1]

Fear and anxiety attack and cripple both our physical and emotional functioning. They also put us into spiritual bondages that hinder our relationship to God. Anxiety and fear are cousins. However, unlike fear, anxiety has no precipitating cause. Fear usually focuses on something, like a frightening event that we must face.

Anxiety can manifest itself in many forms, such as nervousness, excessive tension or a sense of fear that is un-warranted. It often re-sults in sleeplessness, restlessness and an in-ability to concentrate.

> *But those who wait on the LORD will find new strength. They will fly high on wings like eagles. They will run and not grow weary. They will walk and not faint.*
> —ISAIAH 40:31

A common prob-lem in people who have anxiety and panic attacks is an elevated serum lactate level. *Lactate* is sim-ply lactic acid that is formed when blood sugar is broken down anaerobically. *Anaerobic* means "without oxygen."

Therefore, when one is sprinting or exercising at maximum capacity, the blood sugar is broken down into lactic acid, which causes soreness and fatigue in the muscles.

Dr. Melvin Werbach authored a book called *Nutritional Influences on Mental Illness* in which he described the nutritional factors that were responsible for elevated lactate levels.[2]

Glucose is normally broken down to pyruvic acid, which in the presence of oxygen is converted to energy. When pyruvic acid is broken down anaerobically, then lactic acid is produced. High levels of lactic acid are associated with both anxiety and panic attacks.

There are different dietary and nutritional elements associated with high levels of lactic acid. These include increased consumption of sugars, such as sucrose, corn syrup and corn sweeteners; the consumption of caffeine, which includes coffee, colas and tea; and the consumption of alcohol. Alcohol raises lactic acid levels, as will food allergies. The most common food allergies include egg, milk and wheat allergy. A deficiency in B vitamins, calcium and magnesium will also lead to high lactic acid levels. Therefore you should avoid sugar, caffeine and alcohol.

If you have food allergies, I recommend that you decrease or eliminate from your diet all processed starches such as white bread, white flour, white rice, pastries, packaged foods and potato chips. Increase your intake of fruits, vegetables and essential fatty acids such as flaxseed oil, evening primrose oil, black currant oil or fish oil. Drink at least two to three quarts of filtered or distilled water a day.

The Importance of Exercise

One of the best ways to relieve anxiety is to exercise aerobically at least three to four times a week, which includes brisk walking, cycling and swimming. This exercise should last for at least twenty to thirty minutes, and it should be performed at a heart rate between 65 to 80 percent of predicted maximum heart rate. (See the heart rate chart in chapter five of this booklet.)

If you are extremely anxious, you should decrease any activities that create additional stress. For instance, if an outside activity such as a club function or a duty that you must perform leads to too much stress, you should drop it. Relaxation exercises, such as progressive relaxation exercises and deep-breathing exercises, are ways to relax. Avoid volunteering for extra work, and eliminate all unnecessary activities that cause stress.

Meditate on God's Word

Daily meditate on the Word of God, and read aloud scriptures that come against fear and worry. You should pray as often as you are able. You can also purchase a relaxation audiotape at a bookstore.

I recommend that all my patients with anxiety quote scriptures aloud three times a day before meals, meditate on them throughout the day and again quote the scriptures before going to bed.

Pray often, quote scriptures in your prayers and think on the promises of God. Throughout this section of the book are wonderful Bible cure prescriptions for overcoming anxiety. Write them down and memorize them. Put them in places where you can see them—attach sticky notes to your computer or anchor scriptures with magnets on your refrigerator.

The Benefits of Kava

Kava, an herb that comes from islands in the Pacific, is very effective as an anti-anxiety agent, as well as a sedative. The recommended dosage of kava to relieve anxiety is 45 to 90 milligrams, three times a day. Take 135 milligrams at bedtime for insomnia. The dose of kava is based on the level of kavalactones.

Kava does not cause impaired mental function, whereas common anti-anxiety agents such as Xanax, Valium and Ativan can cause impaired mental function. Patients with Parkinson's disease should not take kava since it will worsen their symptoms. Also, excessive amounts of kava can lead to drowsiness and a scaly rash. Kava should not be taken with any other anti-anxiety drugs such as Xanax or Ativan.

Vitamins and Supplements

Patients with anxiety also should take a comprehensive vitamin and mineral supplement like Divine Health Multivitamins and 50 to 100 milligrams of 5-HTP (which is 5-hydroxytryptophan), three times a day. This is also effective in relieving anxiety. You should not take 5-HTP if you are taking any other antidepressant.

Defeating Anxiety Disorders

Anxiety disorders affect women twice as often as men. A panic attack is a severe form of anxiety in which the heart races. Many times the person hyperventilates. He also has sweaty palms and extreme apprehension for no apparent reason. This is simply an adrenaline rush, which is a fight-or-flight reaction that simply occurs at the wrong time.

One of the best ways to prevent a panic attack is to breathe deeply. Inhale slowly through your nose while counting to four. Hold your breath for approximately four seconds; then exhale slowly over a four-second period through your mouth. Continue to do this until the panic attack subsides.

B complex vitamins are very beneficial for anxiety states. Certain herbs are also helpful for reducing anxiety. These include valerian, chamomile, skullcap, hops and passion flower. However, these herbs may cause drowsiness. The normal dose is two to four capsules as needed. Passion flower tea and chamomile tea are helpful for relieving anxiety as well.

Commonly used drugs to treat anxiety include

Xanax, Ativan, Klonopin, Valium and other benzo-diazepenes. These drugs are very addictive, and as many as eighty million prescriptions are written for them each year. These minor tranquilizers numb the human mind. But when the medicine wears off, the person actually becomes more anxious.

For panic disorders, I strongly recommend B-complex vitamins, adrenal glandular supplements and adrenal support. The fight-or-flight response involved with panic attacks commonly drains the adrenal glands. These important glands need to be supported by both vitamins and glandulars.

The Prescription of God's Word

The Word of God is an effective antidote in daily life for both depression and anxiety. God has created natural ways as well as a spiritual prescription for battling and defeating depression and anxiety in your life. In this chapter, you have discovered many positive steps to overcome anxiety. Don't turn back or become discouraged. Continue to move forward with God as you live in His joy and peace.

Memorizing and meditating on Scripture can help tremendously reduce personal anxiety. Throughout this booklet are Bible cure verses. I prescribe one verse a day for you to deposit into your spirit and speak aloud whenever you feel anxiety overcoming you.

The Word of God is an effective antidote in daily life for both depression and anxiety. God has created natural ways as well as a spiritual prescription for battling and defeating depression and anxiety in your life.

> *When you go through deep waters and great trouble, I will be with you. When you go through rivers of difficulty, you will not drown! When you walk through the fire of oppression, you will not be burned up; the flames will not consume you.*
> —ISAIAH 43:2

Overcoming Anxiety

List the steps you take each day to overcome and defeat anxiety and worry:

1. _____

2. _____

3. _____

Review what you have listed. Have you included:

❑ Avoiding caffeine, alcohol and sugar

❑ Meditating on God's Word

❑ Taking kava as needed

❑ Taking a multivitamin

❑ Taking supplements

Chapter 3

Joy-Filled Living
With Proper Nutrition
and Diet

T he things you eat and the things you do can
contribute to feelings of depression. Some of
our most harmful lifestyle and nutritional choices
include drinking alcohol, smoking cigarettes, eating too much sugar, drinking too much caffeine
and eating a diet rich in processed foods such as
white bread, white flour, white rice and pasta.

You can make right nutritional choices today to
replace depression with joy. You may think, *I feel
too depressed to make right choices.* If that's
your thought, then replace it immediately with this:
"For I can do everything with the help of Christ
who gives me the strength I need" (Phil. 4:13).

The delicate balance of chemicals in your brain
is strongly affected when you eat too much protein,

have low blood sugar or high blood sugar (which is diabetes), drink too much caffeine or have critical nutritional deficiencies. All these factors lower your levels of *serotonin,* an important "brain chemical" manufactured by your body that helps your neurons transmit their signals properly. This is why proper lifestyle and dietary choices are critical if you want to prevent depression.

Choose a Healthy Diet

Maintain a balanced diet. A balanced diet includes lots of fruits, vegetables, whole grains, nuts, seeds and lean meats. Take these steps:

- Avoid high-sugar foods such as sodas, desserts, cakes, pies, cookies, candies and cereals.

- Avoid or dramatically decrease processed foods such as bagels, white bread, pretzels, chips, white noodles and the white flour that much of these things are made from (even white rice is a processed food).

- Avoid alcohol, cigarette smoke and caffeine.

SAM-e—the Body's
Amino Acid Antidepressant

The most important methyl donor in the body is SAM-e (a short term for the amino acid S-adenosyl methionine). It is also one of the safest and most effective antidepressants in the world; it has been used in Europe for over twenty years.

SAM-e not only works as an antidepressive with few or no side effects, but it also may improve cognitive function, protect the liver and protect the joints. The usual dose of SAM-e for treating depression ranges from 400 to 1600 milligrams a day, so it can get quite expensive. Fortunately, SAM-e is now available in the vitamin section of Wal-Mart and can be found in retail health food stores as well. I recommend a dose of 200 milligrams two times a day on an empty stomach.

Fatty Acids

Omega-3 fatty acids, such as fish oil and flaxseed oil, can also help prevent the development of depression. Omega-3 fatty acids create strong cell membranes. The brain has the greatest source of fatty acids in the body. For nerve cells to function properly, the brain must have healthy, well-functioning cell membranes. This will directly influence neurotransmitter synthesis and affect levels of serotonin and other neurotransmitters.

I personally take one tablespoon of flaxseed oil twice a day. I also grind five teaspoons of flaxseed in a coffee grinder at least once a day.

So, how do you eat ground flaxseed? You can eat it by the spoonful, add it to cereals or put it in a fruit shake. Another easy way to get flaxseed into your diet is to grind it and add it to the ground meal of muffins, breads and other baked goods. You can replace a few tablespoons of flour in your recipes with ground flaxseed without noticeably changing the taste or texture of your baked goods.

However, don't use flaxseed oil for cooking! Cooking with flaxseed oil oxidizes the oil and forms a very dangerous fat. I keep a bottle of flaxseed oil refrigerated and take one tablespoon twice a day. I throw the bottle out after a month, since it is very prone to oxidation after it has been opened.

Serotonin

I promised earlier to discuss how serotonin can be effective in helping to overcome depression. Serotonin is a type of neurotransmitters, which are chemicals in your brain cells that function as messengers between the nerve endings.

When serotonin levels are low (which can occur when you eat too much sugar or processed foods, smoke cigarettes and drink alcohol and caffeine), then the brain will not function up to par. This will also cause the body not to function at its best.

Serotonin levels in our brains affect our mood, our sleep, whether we develop pain (such as from fibromyalgia) or migraine headaches. Serotonin even affects our appetites. Therefore, not having enough serotonin can lead to depression, anxiety, cravings for certain foods (especially sugars and starches), insomnia and possibly even fibromyalgia and migraine headaches. It also can lead to chronic fatigue syndrome, premenstrual syndrome and even bulimia.

By using brain-imaging techniques, for the first time researchers have seen inadequate serotonin in people who are experiencing depression. Researchers had suspected such a link between depression and serotonin activity for more than a quarter century, but had no direct visual evidence until now.

In a study reported in the *American Journal of Psychiatry,* doctors from the New York State

Psychiatric Institute, Columbia University and the University of Pittsburgh compared six healthy people to six people with major depression who had not been medicated for at least two weeks. Using a serotonin-releasing drug, doctors observed significant increases, as well as decreases, in metabolic activity in the left and right regions of the brain in the healthy patients but not in the patients with depression.[1]

In order for the body to make enough serotonin, it needs tryptophan, which is an essential amino acid. Vegetarians may not have adequate amounts of tryptophan in their diets unless they practice proper nutrition in combining protein foods to form complete proteins.

A BIBLE CURE HEALTHFACT

Foods That Fight Depression

Good sources of tryptophan include the following:

- Turkey
- Eggs
- Almonds
- Chicken
- Soybeans
- Milk products

Food Allergies and Depression

Food allergies have also been linked to depression. I have found in my practice that many people are either allergic or sensitive to eggs, milk, wheat, corn and soybeans—to name only a few of the most common allergens.

When patients are allergic to corn, they are usually also allergic to vitamin C, since practically all vitamin C is made from corn. Therefore, they do not get the full benefit of this powerful antioxidant.

If you happen to be allergic to wheat, you also may be allergic to the B-complex vitamins, and you may not effectively utilize these important vitamins. This allergy or sensitivity can lead to fatigue and depression.

If you are experiencing depression and also have food allergies, I believe that it is critically important to desensitize from these foods (or in other words, to no longer be sensitive to them) in order to overcome the depression. One of the best methods I have found is N.A.E.T., which is a form of allergy desensitization using acupuncture. I have seen hundreds of patients desensitized from food allergies by using this technique.

The Effects of Antidepressants

The most commonly prescribed antidepressant on the market is Prozac. Prozac causes the brain to have increased levels of serotonin by preventing its reuptake by the brain cells. The brain is able to use its serotonin for longer periods of time, which leads to a nondepressed mood.

Prozac and the other SSRIs, which include Zoloft and Paxil, only prevent the reuptake of serotonin and do nothing about increasing the supply of other neurotransmitters as 5-HTP does. These drugs are also known to have side effects, which include loss or decrease of sex drive, nausea and vomiting, fatigue, anxiety, agitation, insomnia, diarrhea, headaches, sweating tremors, skin rashes and drowsiness.

Prozac and other antidepressants can also cause sexual dysfunction, which includes the inability to either achieve or sustain an erection in men and the inability to achieve orgasm in both men and women. If you are on any of these medications, do not make any changes without first consulting with your physician.

We have explored how proper nutrition can help us move from depression to joy-filled living.

As you determine to eat right, pray for the strength to choose the right foods.

A BIBLE CURE PRAYER
FOR YOU

Almighty God, empower me spiritually to take control over my appetite so that what I eat helps my body overcome depression. Remove from me the desire for foods and thoughts that fuel depression. Fill me with Your Spirit so that I may discern and decide to eat and think right so that your Spirit of joy will replace any spiritual heaviness in me. Amen.

A BIBLE CURE PRESCRIPTION

Your Diet to Overcome Depression

In this chapter we have discovered that certain foods can help us overcome depression. Check which of the following foods you will begin including regularly in your diet:

- ❏ Turkey
- ❏ Chicken
- ❏ Eggs
- ❏ Soybeans
- ❏ Almonds
- ❏ Milk products
- ❏ Fish and flaxseed oil

Write a prayer asking God to help you use proper nutrition to fight depression:

_____

_____

_____

_____

_____

_____

Chapter 4

Joy-Filled Living
With Vitamins and
Minerals

G od has created wonderful natural substances that can help you overcome depression: vitamins, minerals, amino acids and herbs. These powerful substances are readily available in pharmacies and health food stores. Although they are no substitute for consulting a physician or professional counseling, they will help you to overcome depression.

The best place to start in treating depression is to begin taking a comprehensive vitamin and mineral formula, like Divine Health Multivitamins. A comprehensive multivitamin supplement helps to reduce your risk of developing depression. (Unfortunately, most over-the-counter multivitamins and minerals are lacking in optimal amounts of certain vitamin and minerals. Those they do have are often in a form that is virtually indigestable, so it is wise to pay a little more for better grade vitamins like Divine Health Multivitamins.)

Medical and nutritional researchers often find that entire groups of test subjects with a common disease or affliction also share an obvious vitamin deficiency. This may indicate that the missing vitamin has properties that are able to ward off or diminish the symptoms of the particular disease or affliction. Researchers have found that depressed patients are commonly deficient in B_6, B_{12} and folic acid. All of these function as "methyl donors," which are absolutely necessary for human neurotransmitters to function efficiently.

I recommend a low dose of 5-HTP, 50 milligrams, three times a day with meals, eventually working up to 100 milligrams three times a day with meals. However, do *not* take 5-HTP with any other antidepressants. In addition to multivitamins and 5-HTP, I also place my patients on good antioxidants, ones that contain significant amounts of the following:

- Vitamin E (800 I.U. a day)
- Vitamin C (1000 mg. two to three times a day)

- Grape seed extract (50 mg. one to two times a day)
- Pine bark extract (50 mg. one to two times a day)
- Selenium (200 mcg. a day)
- Beta carotene (25,000 I.U. a day)
- Vitamin A (5000 I.U. a day)
- Coenzyme Q_{10} (50 mg. one to two times a day)
- Lipoic acid (50 mg. one to two times a day)

A combination of these antioxidants offers much more protection from free-radical reactions than any single antioxidant, since the antioxidants seem to recycle one another. If your antioxidant levels are high, it may help you to maintain high serotonin levels.

Often vitamin B_6 levels are also low in individuals who are depressed, especially in women on birth control pills. B_6 is critical in the formation of serotonin. To insure you have adequate amounts of B_6, as well as the other important B vitamins, take approximately 800 micrograms of folic acid, 1000 micrograms of B_{12} and 100 milligrams of B_6.

Acetyl-L-Carnitine

Another nutrient that may affect depression is

acetyl-l-carnitine, which is an amino acid. Acetyl-1-carnitine, taken in a dose of 1000 milligrams two times a day, may improve cognitive functioning and help to alleviate depression. This nutrient also helps the body to resist aging.

St. John's Wort is an herb that has been used in Germany for many years to treat depression. It is actually the first choice in therapy for the treatment of depression in Germany. It is prescribed more often than any other antidepressant, including Prozac. St. John's Wort has very mild side effects and no serious drug interactions.

Like Prozac, St. John's Wort inhibits serotonin reuptake. St. John's Wort also can help you sleep better. The brand of St. John's Wort you purchase should have a 0.3 percent hypericin content. The standard dose is 300 milligrams three times a day. Do not take St. John's Wort with any other antidepressants.

L-tyrosine is an amino acid that is eventually converted to dopamine, norepinephrine and epinephrine, which are neurotransmitters. The dose of L-tyrosine is 500 to 1500 milligrams a day.

D,L-phenylalanine is another amino acid that is converted to tyrosine and leads to the production of neurotransmitters. Both tyrosine and phenylalanine have mood-elevating properties and may be beneficial along with 5-HTP. The dose of D,L-phenylalanine is two 500-milligram capsules in the morning on an empty stomach and one 500-milligram capsule later in the afternoon on an empty stomach.

Ginkgo biloba is an herb that has been used for many years in treating memory loss and cerebral vascular insufficiency, which is simply decreased blood flow to the brain. Ginkgo is also a remarkable antidepressant. An aging brain will have a decreasing number of serotonin receptor sites. Thus, aging individuals are very prone to develop depression and sleep disturbances. Ginkgo biloba, however, prevents or slows down the loss of serotonin receptor sites. Also, ginkgo biloba is very safe; there is no interaction between ginkgo and other antidepressants. The normal dose of ginkgo biloba is 100 milligrams three times a day.

5-HTP

In the 1990s it was discovered that 5-HTP (hydroxy tryptophan) was another amino acid closely related to tryptophan. However, it is a step closer to the formation of serotonin. It was also found that 5-HTP is superior to tryptophan and very safe. This amino acid is derived from the seed of the *griffonia simplicifolia* plant from Africa. Its processing does not involve fermentation, and the seed is a natural source.

What Is 5-HTP?

Briefly, 5-HTP is a chemical cousin to tryptophan, an essential aminio acid found in protein. Tryptophan is a precursor, or building block, of 5-HTP, which in turn is ultimately converted to serotonin. Protein foods such as milk and poultry are rich sources of tryptophan. A lack of tryptophan flowing into the brain can result in depression, increased sensitivity to pain and wakefulness.[1]

It is not necessary to take as high a dose of 5-HTP as tryptophan since more of it is delivered to the brain. Also, 5-HTP is able to raise the level of all monoamine neurotransmitters, which include norepinephrine, epinephrine, dopamine, melatonin and serotonin.

Serotonin, however, is absolutely critical for

optimal brain functioning. Serotonin also helps us to feel both calm and relaxed, as well as helps us stay alert, energetic, happy and well rested. The normal dose of 5-HTP is 50 milligrams three times a day with meals. However, after a couple of weeks, you may increase the dose to 100 milligrams three times a day with meals. You should not take 5-HTP with any other antidepressants, such as Prozac, Zoloft and Paxil.

Kava is an herb that has been used for centuries in the islands of the Pacific such as Polynesia. Kava has been used for treating anxiety, but it also has been found to be very effective in treating mixed anxiety and depression. It is not uncommon for depressed patients to experience both anxiety

> *All praise to the God and Father of our Lord Jesus Christ. He is the source of every mercy and the God who comforts us. He comforts us in all our troubles so that we can comfort others. When others are troubled, we will be able to give them the same comfort God has given us.*
> —2 CORINTHIANS 1:3–4

and depression at the same time. Kava has been approved in certain European countries, including Great Britain, for the treatment of anxiety and depression. Kava is nonaddictive and does not decrease mental functioning like other anti-anxiety drugs, which include Xanax and Valium.

Kava is normally taken in a dose of approximately 45 to 90 milligrams of kavalactones three times a day.

Passion flower is an herb that has been used for centuries as a sedative. It is also used commonly in Germany for restlessness. The normal dose is 100 to 300 milligrams at bedtime of a 2.6 percent standardized extract.

Depression and the Thyroid Gland

Low thyroid function also can lead to depression, as can low estrogen and progesterone levels in females.

This is commonly seen when women are in menopause. Many women develop signs and symptoms of depression that are totally alleviated when they start estrogen and progesterone replacement

> *Don't be afraid, for I am with you. Do not be dismayed, for I am your God. I will strengthen you. I will help you. I will uphold you with my righteous right hand.*
> —Isaiah 41:10

therapy. I prefer that my patients use the natural estrogen and progesterone hormones.

Toxins Lead to Depression

Our world is very toxic. We are exposed daily to toxins in our food, water and air. Heavy metals such as lead, cadmium, mercury, arsenic and aluminum are ingested daily in our food, water and even in the air we breathe. Solvents such as isopropyl alcohol, benzene, formaldehyde and cleaning materials are being absorbed through our skin and being stored in our fatty tissues. We also are exposed daily to pesticides and herbicides due to the produce and fatty foods that we eat on a daily basis. Pesticides are easily stored in fatty tissue.

On a daily basis, our bodies are accumulating a heavier and heavier toxic burden due to our constant exposure to these toxins. These toxins are stored in our fatty tissues, our nervous tissue, bones and organs. They create such a toxic burden that we eventually develop fatigue and depression. (You can learn more about detoxification in *The Bible Cure for Cancer* booklet.)

The Effects of Caffeine and Sugar

Caffeine and excessive sugar intake also have been linked to depression. Most Americans drink carbonated beverages that are high in sugar and caffeine. We also drink quite a bit of coffee and tea and usually add sugar to these beverages. Excessive caffeine and sugar intake will eventually lead to a loss in B vitamins, an increase in the stress hormone cortisol and sleep disturbances.

These nutrient deficiencies, along with an excess of cortisol and inadequate sleep, can eventually lead to depression.

> *And I will give you a new heart with new and right desires, and I will put a new spirit in you. I will take out your stony heart of sin and give you a new, obedient heart.*
> —EZEKIEL 36:26

As you overcome depression with joy, use God-created vitamins and supplements to help your body throw off any spirit of heaviness. Before you take your vitamins and supplements, pray over them. In doing so, God's blessing and anointing can empower what is natural in a supernatural way to be even more effective in physically strengthening you.

A BIBLE CURE PRAYER
FOR YOU

Almighty God, You have created these vitamins and the substances for these supplements. Before I take them, I pray for Your Spirit to impart potency to them for helping me physically. Speed each essential substance to the precise cell that needs it. Fill my body, soul and spirit with your joy that no circumstance can rob. Amen.

R A BIBLE CURE PRESCRIPTION

Overcoming Depression
With Vitamins and Supplements

Circle the vitamins, minerals and supplements you take regularly and underline those you plan to begin taking:

5-HTP	Vitamin C	Vitamin E
St. John's Wort	Grape seed extract	Pine bark extract
Selenium	Beta carotene	Vitamin A
Coenzyme Q_{10}	Lipoic acid	Gingko biloba
Passion flower	Kava	L-tyrosine
	D,L-phenylalanine	

Will you limit your daily caffeine intake?

❏ Yes ❏ No

Describe how:

_____

_____

_____

Will you limit your daily sugar intake?

❏ Yes ❏ No

Chapter 5

Joy-Filled Living With Exercise and Rest

Exercise is the absolute best natural antidepressant. Studies have shown that exercise and sports are associated with decreases in both depression and anxiety. One of the main reasons active individuals feel better is that exercise releases endorphins into the body and brain. Endorphins are morphine-like compounds that elevate an individual's mood.[1]

Some individuals get so depressed that that they have no energy to exercise. In these cases I recommend starting immediately on either

> *He gives power to those who are tired and worn out; he offers strength to the weak.*
> —Isaiah 40:29

5-HTP, St. John's Wort or SAM-e.

I recommend that all my patients exercise at least three to four times a week for at least twenty minutes aerobically. This includes brisk walking, swimming, cycling, stair-stepping, aerobics or the Precor gliding machine. I personally prefer the Precor gliding machine since there is no strain on the joints.

I also recommend that you purchase a heart rate monitor so you can train within your own training heart rate zone. If you are exercising aerobically, purchase a heart rate monitor at a sporting goods store.

Then calculate your target heart rate zone. Your heart rate zone should be 60 to 80 percent of the predicted maximum heart rate.

> *And I am convinced that nothing can ever separate us from his love. Death can't, and life can't. The angels can't, and the demons can't. Our fears for today, our worries about tomorrow, and even the powers of hell can't keep God's love away. Whether we are high above the sky or in the deepest ocean, nothing in all creation will ever be able to separate us from the love of God that is revealed in Christ Jesus our Lord.*
> —ROMANS 8:38–39

Your Predicted Heart
Rate for Exercise

To calculate your target heart zone, follow the formula below:

220 minus [your age] = _____ x .65 = _____
[This is your minimum.]
220 minus [your age] = _____ x .80 = _____
[This is your maximum.]

For example, to calculate the target heart zone for a forty-year-old man, subtract his age (40) from 220 (220- 40=180). Multiply 180 by .65, which equals 117. Then multiply 180 by .80, which equals 144. Therefore, a forty-year old man's target heart rate zone is 117–144 beats per minute.

A heart rate monitor goes around the chest, and a wristwatch monitors the heart rate. The forty-year-old man would then be able to keep his heart rate between 117 and 144. This would oxygenate all the tissues in the body and raise the levels of endorphins that prevent or alleviate depression.

HEALTHFACT HEALTHFACT HEALTHFACT HEALTHFACT HEALTHFACT HEALTHFACT HEALTHFACT

The Importance of Sleep

Sleep is extremely important in overcoming depression. Restful sleep leads to improved immune function, improved mood, a more youthful appearance, improved stamina, improved mental function and improved memory. Sleep deprivation leads to a decrease in immune function.

Sleep deprivation may be one of the reasons we are seeing an epidemic in cancer. As many as 40 percent of the population will develop cancer at some time in their lives. During the sleeping hours is when our body repairs its damaged tissues. If our body doesn't have time to repair these damaged or worn-out tissues, the end result is often disease.

> *And this same God who takes care of me will supply all your needs from his glorious riches, which have been given to us in Christ Jesus.*
> —PHILIPPIANS 4:19

Adults need about seven to eight hours of sleep at night—this is even true for elderly individuals. Elderly people can have trouble sleeping well at night because they do not have the same serotonin levels of younger individuals. Approximately one out of three people have insomnia on a regular basis.

Insomnia is simply the inability to fall asleep and remain asleep during the night. Since insomnia frequently leads to depression, it is critically important to correct this disorder.

> *For the law was given through Moses; God's unfailing love and faithfulness came through Jesus Christ.*
> —JOHN 1:17

The first step in correcting insomnia is to maintain a diet that is free of caffeine, chocolate and other stimulants. Caffeine inhibits the effects of serotonin and melatonin in the brain and also activates both the nerves and muscles, getting the heart pumping faster.

Alcohol is another toxic chemical that prevents an individual from getting a good night's sleep. In addition, avoid exercising too late in the evening or near bedtime since this will stimulate instead of relax the body. Never watch action-packed movies before bedtime, since they too can get your adrenaline flowing. Before falling asleep, try the following:

- Practice relaxation techniques such as progressive relaxation at bedtime. Relax while lying in bed. Begin by flexing the toes for one to two seconds and then relaxing them. Then systematically flex and relax the muscles all the way up to your head.
- Eat a small meal prior to bedtime if you are prone to developing low blood sugar. Enjoy a light snack consisting of 40 percent carbohydrates, 30 percent protein and 30 percent fat.
- Empty your bladder before going to bed so you do not awaken in the middle of the night and then find it difficult to fall back asleep.
- If you have tried all the basic steps outlined above and still find it difficult to fall asleep, take 100–300 milligrams of 5-HTP approximately thirty minutes to an hour before retiring. You may also take valerian and passion flower in a dose of 300 milligrams each approximately an hour before bedtime. You might also try 1–3

milligrams of melatonin thirty minutes to an hour prior to bedtime. Also, use prayer and reading Scripture as God's way to calm your spirit and instill you with His peace.

In this chapter, we have focused on the importance of physical exercise and adequate rest. However, the Bible cure affirms the benefits of *both physical and spiritual exercise* for our continuing health. The Bible says, "Physical exercise has some value, but spiritual exercise is much more important, for it promises a reward in both this life and the next. This is true, and everyone should accept it" (1 Tim. 4:8–9). As you exercise your faith, trusting God to remove pain, strengthen and heal your body, you will boldly pray for your healing.

> *So humble yourselves under the mighty power of God, and in his good time he will honor you. Give all your worries and cares to God, for he cares about what happens to you.*
> —1 Peter 5:6–7

I have explained to you the physical benefits of exercise in overcoming depression; now let me share with you the spiritual benefits of exercising your faith and boldly praying for your healing. God's Word encourages us to "come boldly to the throne of our gracious God. There we will receive his mercy, and we will find grace to help us when we need it" (Heb. 4:16).

You can boldly approach God's throne in prayer. How?

- Believe in faith, trusting God the Healer for your healing.

- Trust His promises to heal you. For example, "He [God] sent his word, and healed them, and delivered them from their destructions" (Ps. 107:20, KJV).

- Pray boldly for your healing, knowing that in His mercy and grace, God's will for you is to walk in divine health.

- Ask God to give you rest and peace. Jesus said, "Come to me, all of you who are weary and carry heavy burdens, and I will give you rest. Take my yoke upon you. Let me teach you, because I am humble and gentle, and you will find rest for your souls" (Matt. 11:28–29).

A BIBLE CURE PRAYER
FOR YOU

Almighty God, in the name of Jesus and through His shed blood, I boldly approach Your throne of grace and seek Your healing power and touch. I know that by Jesus' stripes I have been healed. I claim Your promise that you have forgiven all my sins and healed all my diseases. So I boldly stand on Your promises of healing, and I praise You for helping me to overcome depression with joy. In the name of Jesus, amen.

A BIBLE CURE PRESCRIPTION

Overcoming Depression

Do you:

- ❑ Rarely exercise
- ❑ Exercise occasionally
- ❑ Exercise regularly

If you are not exercising regularly, when will you start? What exercise program will you implement?

_____

_____

How many hours a night are you sleeping? How many should you be sleeping? If you are not getting enough sleep, what will you do about it?

_____

_____

Check the steps you need to start taking before you fall asleep at night:

- ❑ Practice relaxation techniques
- ❑ Eat a light snack before bedtime
- ❑ Take 5-HTP if necessary

Chapter 6

Joy-Filled
Living With the
Word of God

As a physician, I am trained to carefully examine my patients and prescribe any medicines or lifestyle changes that may be necessary. I have found that my *most powerful prescription for healthy living* can't be found in a bottle or at a pharmacist's counter. It has one exclusive source, and it is freely available to everyone. I am talking about the Word of God, of course. Joy and peace can come to even the most troubled minds when people discover new ways of looking at life based upon the truth of God's wonderful Word.

Most depressed people have a very pessimistic attitude and are constantly beating themselves down with their thoughts, words and attitudes. Depressed people are usually in a pessimistic rut of negative thoughts that they cannot break out of on their own. That is why I believe it is absolutely essential for people battling depression to begin rewiring their negative thoughts with the Word of God. These biblical "self-talks" are extremely important in overcoming depression.

How do I begin? Begin to read scriptures aloud at least three times a day—before you eat your meals and at bedtime. Whenever a negative thought comes to mind, quote a scripture aloud to break the habit of negative thinking.

> *Those who have been ransomed by the LORD will return to Jerusalem, singing songs of everlasting joy. Sorrow and mourning will disappear, and they will be overcome with joy and gladness.*
> —ISAIAH 51:11

Throughout this booklet, I have inserted selected portions from the Bible as your Bible cure verses for overcoming depression. Before falling asleep at night, repeat or pray these scriptures. Do so again when you awake.

One person I know has written these scriptures on three-by-five cards and put them in his pocket. Each day he pulls out his scripture cards and reads each scripture aloud to fill his mind with hope and joy. You can overcome depression with God's Word and by taking the various steps suggested throughout this book. *Don't quit. Don't give up.* God's hope and joy are available to fill you and defeat every spirit of heaviness in your life. Pray this Bible cure prayer as you overcome depression:

A BIBLE CURE PRAYER
FOR YOU

Heavenly Father, I know that You love and care for me. I pray that You will remove any spirit of heaviness from my life. Please clothe me with the garments of praise and joy.

Lord, help me to know which vitamins, supplements and herbs to take that will help my body fight depression. Give me rest and strength as I seek Your will in my life. Father God, remove the weight of grief, depression and sadness from my life. Help me to remember Your Word as I seek wisdom and guidance in overcoming every aspect of depression in my life. I trust You, and I know that Your Word is true. Lord Jesus, You said that Your purpose was to give life in all its fullness. I thank You in advance for releasing this fullness in my life. In Your name I pray these things with thanksgiving and praise. Amen.

Speak Uplifting and Encouraging Words

You may not want to admit it, but you probably talk to yourself from time to time. Don't worry; it is very normal. In fact, the most important conversations that we have are those we have with ourselves! Unfortunately, people who are depressed tend to have mostly negative con-

> *Dear friends, don't be surprised at the fiery trials you are going through . . . Instead, be very glad—because these trials will make you partners with Christ in his suffering, and afterward you will have the wonderful joy of sharing his glory. . . .*
> —1 PETER 4:12–13

versations with themselves. This makes things even worse because it means their minds are constantly barraged by nagging negative thoughts that beat them down a little lower each day.

I have seen fathers at Little League baseball games constantly criticizing their children, calling them stupid, dumb, pitiful—saying that they can't do anything right. I have seen the poor children standing in the outfield or slumped over sitting on the bench with a dejected, depressed look on their little faces. Unfortunately, some of these children who have been told that they are losers, that they are dumb, stupid and can never do anything right, grow up to believe those words.

> *The Spirit of the Sovereign LORD is upon me, because the LORD has appointed me to bring good news to the poor. He has sent me to comfort the brokenhearted and to announce that captives will be released and prisoners will be freed. He has sent me to tell those who mourn that the time of the LORD's favor has come, and with it, the day of God's anger against their enemies. To all who mourn in Israel, he will give beauty for ashes, joy instead of mourning, praise instead of despair. For the LORD has planted them like strong and graceful oaks for his own glory.*
> —ISAIAH 61:1–3

They become depressed, unmotivated and unsuccessful people.

If a person feeds on negative thoughts throughout the day, every task or every trial that comes his way will be approached from a defeated attitude before he even undertakes it. However, we have the ability, through the Word of God, to *speak* God's Word throughout

> *Go and celebrate with a feast of choice foods and sweet drinks, and share gifts of food with people who have nothing prepared. This is a sacred day before our Lord. Don't be dejected and sad, for the joy of the LORD is your strength!*
> —NEHEMIAH 8:10

the day and rewire these negative thoughts into positive thoughts, which will then bring healing and health to the body and the mind.

Thinking Joyful Thoughts

It is critically important for a depressed patient to train the mind to think positive thoughts rather than dwelling on the negative. When a negative thought pops into the mind, it is important to cast down that thought and to speak out the solution, which is the Word of God. That is why quoting scriptures is so important. Biblical and positive thoughts lead to winning attitudes.

67

An attitude is a choice. A person can choose to have a negative attitude, or he can choose to have a positive attitude. You can choose to be angry, bitter, resentful, unforgiving, fearful or ashamed. These negative attitudes eventually affect our health and allow diseases to take root in our bodies.

Avoid Resentment
and Unforgiveness

Resentment and unforgiveness are commonly associated with arthritis, whereas fear is commonly associated with cancer. Anxiety is commonly associated with ulcers, and anger is very commonly associated with heart disease. These are deadly emotions. If they are not taken out of us through the Word of God or with the help of a trained professional, they can eventually lead to disease.

When Paul and Silas were placed in prison in Acts 16:23, they prayed and sang praises. Paul had a choice. He could have had a negative attitude and become angry, resentful and bitter. Instead, he chose to rejoice and sing praises. He chose the healthy attitude. He decided to "rejoice always" (1 Thess. 5:16, NAS).

When an individual wrongs you, it is very easy to hold bitterness, resentment, anger and unforgiveness. However, this works against your body and will actually cause disease to set in. It is far better for your body—for both your mental and physical health—to forgive the person and release these deadly emotions before they take root in your mind and body.

> *Wherever he went—in villages and cities and out on the farms—they laid the sick in the market plazas and streets. The sick begged him to let them at least touch the fringe of his robe, and all who touched it were healed.*
> —Mark 6:56

The Bible says it plainly: "Do not let the sun go down on your anger" (Eph. 4:26, NAS). This, I believe, is one of the most important keys in preventing these deadly emotions from locking onto our minds and bodies and eventually killing us.

Paul wrote that he decided to forget those things that were behind him and to press forward to the prize of the mark of the high calling in

Christ Jesus. (See Philippians 3:14.) Choose the right attitude as soon as you wake up in the morning. When someone wrongs you, forgive that person immediately. Do not focus on the wrong.

Our thoughts lead to the words we say, and our words lead to our attitudes. It is critically important to

> *He heals the broken-hearted, binding up their wounds.*
> —Psalm 147:3

guard our thoughts and to quote the Word of God aloud throughout the day in order to produce godly attitudes within us. This is one of the most important points in preventing depression. Nutrition, exercise and adequate sleep are all important. However, our thoughts, words and attitudes will determine if we succeed or if we fail; they determine where we spend our eternity as well.

Your Favorite Scriptures

Write out three of your favorite scriptures for fighting depression:

_____

_____

_____

_____

_____

_____

_____

Circle one choice as to where you are and a check on the line where you need to be:

_____

Negative thinker   Positive Thinker

_____

Resentful   Forgiving

Notes

CHAPTER 1
JOY INSTEAD OF SADNESS

1. J. R. Davidson, et. al. "The underrecognition and undertreatment of depression: what is the breadth and depth of the problem?" *J Clin Psychiatry* (1999); 60 Suppl 7:4–9; discussion 10–1. Review. PMID: 10326869; UI: 99256801.

2. Adapted from materials created by the National Institute of Mental Health's Depression Awareness, Recognition and Treatment (D/ART) Program, Rockville, Maryland.

3. Adapted from the "Social Readjustment Rating Scale" by Thomas Holmes and Richard Rahe. This scale was first published in the *Journal of Psychosomatic Research,* copyright 1967, Vol. II, 214.

4. Adapted from Carol Watkins, M.D., "Depression in Children and Adolescents," Obtained from Internet Source. Northern County Psychiatric Associates, Lutherville and Monkton, Baltimore County, Maryland, Web site www.ncpamd.com.

5. M. E. P. Seligmann and J. B. Overmier. "Effects of Inescapable Shock Upon Subsequent Escape and Avoidance Responding," *Journal of Comparative and Physiological Psychology* (1967), 63, 28 38.

6. J. Mendlewicz, ed. *Management of Depression with Monoamine Precursors* (n.p.: S. Karger Publishing, 1983). Obtained from Internet source.

Chapter 2

Peace Instead of Anxiety

1. Matthew Naythons, M.D., and the staff of NetHealth, publisher of the Internet *Health Fitness, and Medicine Yellow Pages* (Osborne McGraw Hill). NetHealth is a division of Epicenter Communications, Inc., of Sausalito, California. Source obtained from the Internet.

2. Dr. Melvin Werbach, *Nutritional Influences on Mental Illness* (Keats Publishing, 2nd ed., 1996). Source obtained from the Internet.

Chapter 3

Joy-Filled Living With Proper Nutrition and Diet

1. National Alliance for the Mentally Ill, "Impaired Serotonin Activity Can Be Seen in People With Depression," reporting on a study in the *American Journal of Psychiatry,* February 1999.

Chapter 4

Joy-Filled Living With Vitamins and Minerals

1. Dean Wolfe Manders, Ph.D., "The FDA Ban of L-Tryptophan: Politics, Profits and Prozac," *Social Policy,* Vol. 26, No. 2, Winter (1995).

Chapter 5

Joy-Filled Living With Exercise and Rest

1. Robert A. Roberts and Scott O. Roberts, *Exercise Physiology: Exercise, Performance and Clinical Applications* (n.p.: McGraw-Hill, 1996) (Internet source).

Don Colbert, M.D., was born in Tupelo, Mississippi. He attended Oral Roberts School of Medicine in Tulsa, Oklahoma, where he received a bachelor of science degree in biology in addition to his degree in medicine. Dr. Colbert completed his internship and residency with Florida Hospital in Orlando, Florida. He is board certified in family practice and has received extensive training in nutritional medicine.

If you would like more
information about natural and
divine healing, or information about
Divine Health Nutritional Products®,
you may contact
Dr. Colbert at:

DR. DON COLBERT

1908 Boothe Circle
Longwood, FL 32750
Telephone: 407-331-7007

Dr. Colbert's website is
www.drcolbert.com.

BIBLE CURE

NOTES

_____

_____

_____

_____

_____

_____

_____

_____

_____

_____

_____

_____

_____

BIBLE CURE

NOTES

_____
_____
_____
_____
_____
_____
_____
_____
_____
_____
_____
_____

BIBLE CURE

BIBLE CURE

NOTES

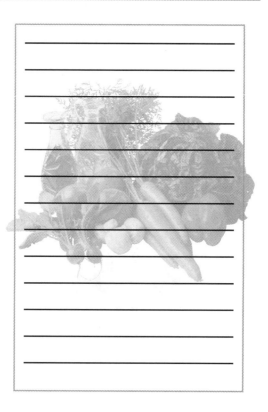

_____
_____
_____
_____
_____
_____
_____
_____
_____
_____
_____
_____
_____

BIBLE CURE

NOTES

_____
_____
_____
_____
_____
_____
_____
_____
_____
_____
_____
_____

BIBLE CURE

NOTES

_____

_____

_____

_____

_____

_____

_____

_____

_____

_____

_____

_____

_____

BIBLE CURE

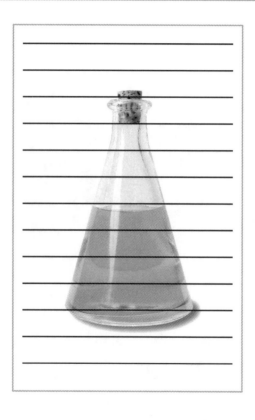

BIBLE CURE

NOTES

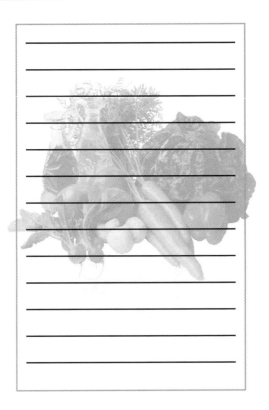

BIBLE CURE

NOTES

BIBLE CURE

NOTES

Your Favorite Scriptures

Write out three of your favorite scriptures for fighting depression:

_____

_____

_____

_____

_____

_____

_____

Circle one choice as to where you are and a check on the line where you need to be:

_____

Negative thinker   Positive Thinker

_____

Resentful   Forgiving

Pick up these other Siloam Press
books by Dr. Colbert:

Walking in Divine Health
What You Don't Know May Be Killing You
Toxic Relief

The Bible Cure® Booklet Series

The Bible Cure for ADD and Hyperactivity
The Bible Cure for Allergies
The Bible Cure for Arthritis
The Bible Cure for Cancer
The Bible Cure for Candida and Yeast Infection
The Bible Cure for Chronic Fatigue and Fibromyalgia
The Bible Cure for Depression and Anxiety
The Bible Cure for Diabetes
The Bible Cure for Headaches
The Bible Cure for Heart Disease
The Bible Cure for Heartburn and Indigestion
The Bible Cure for High Blood Pressure
The Bible Cure for Memory Loss
The Bible Cure for Menopause
The Bible Cure for Osteoporosis
The Bible Cure for PMS and Mood Swings
The Bible Cure for Sleep Disorders
The Bible Cure for Weight Loss and Muscle Gain

SILOAM PRESS

A part of Strang Communications Company
600 Rinehart Road
Lake Mary, FL 34726
(800) 599-5750